# "I Am A Little Bored."

~

By Francesca Steffey

I am a little bored.

You ARE?

Yes, I am a little bored.

What kind of board are you?

Are you an ironing board?

Are you good under pressure, help to straighten things out, and leave things looking fresher?

## No. 1-

Oh! Are you a snowboard?

Cruising down a snowy hill? Sounds chilly!

No, no. I said I -

Maybe you are a surfboard!

Hang 10, Cool dude!

Say hello, to the next gnarly wave for me!

No, No, NO! I am just-

Hmmm.

Perhaps that is not your speed? Are you a Paddle Board?

Paddling along, exploring lakes and calm seas?

Oh. My. Goodness.
No, you are not listening. I am-

What? What!? A fancy cheeseboard?

Do you have any samples? That would be real gouda!

Um, no...

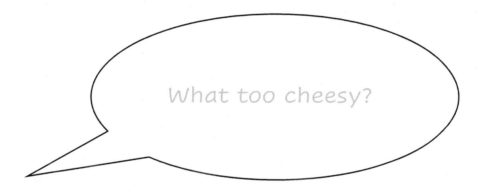

Oh brother. No, I am just-

Just what?
A chalkboard, a whiteboard?
Oh, I know what you are!
You are a bulletin board, right?
How excellent! I use mine for posting photos!
Do you want to take a selfie with me?

You know...
I cannot do this ANY more!

You are making me go
# CUCKOO!

# YES, CUCKOO!

What kind of board—

OH!

I am sorry, I misunderstood you!

Silly me.

You did not say you were a little board,

did you?

Well, not exactly I-

You have been trying to tell me this WHOLE

time.

I should have listened, but I understand now.

...

You do?

Yes!

You said you are a little BIRD!!

CUCKOO!

(eye roll)

Cuckoo.

# The End.

Made in the USA
Monee, IL
30 May 2024

59082805R00017